Use cubes to subtract. Match each boat to an island.

Write a subtraction story on this boat.

Amy and Jack go to Mango Island.
How much has each left?

Amy ____ p

Jack ____ p

3

To land on the island, find numbers which add to 11.

Use counters.

| $10 + 1$ | | | | |
| | | | | |

How many 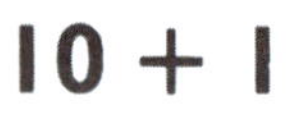? ___
3 fly away.

$11 - 3 = $ ___

How many ? ___
7 fall off.

$11 - 7 = $ ___

How many ? ___
5 are picked.

$11 - 5 = $ ___

How many ? ___
9 hide.

$11 - 9 = $ ___

Islands

Use cubes to add.

Use pennies. How much is it to go to

Mango Island and Nim-Nam-Noo ⬚ p

Nim-Nam-Noo and Bear Island ⬚ p ?

HEINEMANN MATHEMATICS 2

Name

WORKBOOK 4

Addition and Subtraction to 13, Halves and Quarters

Bushes

Each bush has 11 flowers.   Write stories.

$9 + 2 = 11$

$2 + 9 = 11$

$11 - 2 = 9$

$11 - 9 = 2$

$8 + 3 =$

$3 + 8 =$

$11 - 3 =$

$11 - 8 =$

$7 + 4 =$

$4 + 7 =$

$11 - 4 =$

$11 - 7 =$

$6 + 5 =$

$5 + 6 =$

$11 - 5 =$

$11 - 6 =$

Find sets of 3 numbers which add to 11.

$5 + 3 + 3$

+ and − facts for 11
5
In the jungle
4
+7
11
−3
3
+8
11
−9
11
−6
11 − 4 =
11 − 8 =
5 + 6 =
11 − 2 =
11 − 1 =
The nest has 11 eggs.
4 fall out.
How many left?
11 flies
5 ants
How many
more flies?
3 + 4 + 4 =
5 + 2 + 3 =
Food
R 20

Buying food

How much does each spend?

Each child has 11p.   They buy these things.
How much has each left?

Spend 11p.
What 3 things will you buy?

R 21

Nim-Nam-Noo

Put 12 Nim-nams on the island like this.

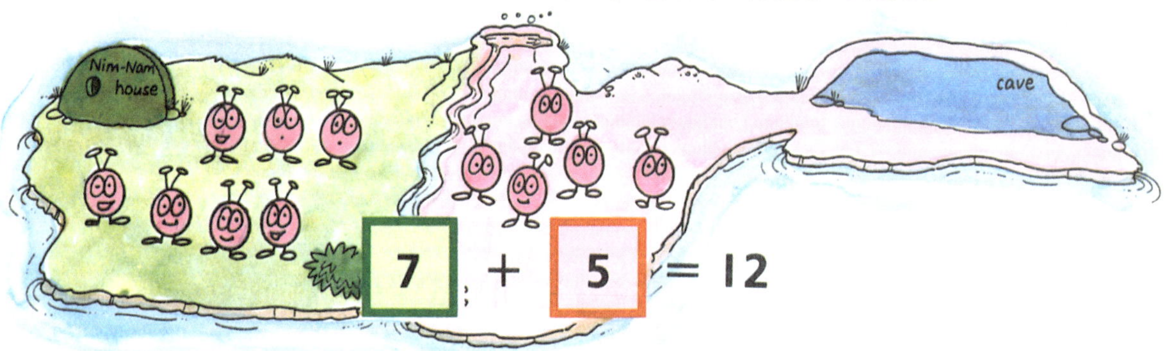

Find other ways to put 12 Nim-nams on the island.

☐ + ☐ = 12   ☐ + ☐ = 12

☐ + ☐ = 12   ☐ + ☐ = 12

☐ + ☐ = 12   ☐ + ☐ = 12

☐ + ☐ = 12   ☐ + ☐ = 12

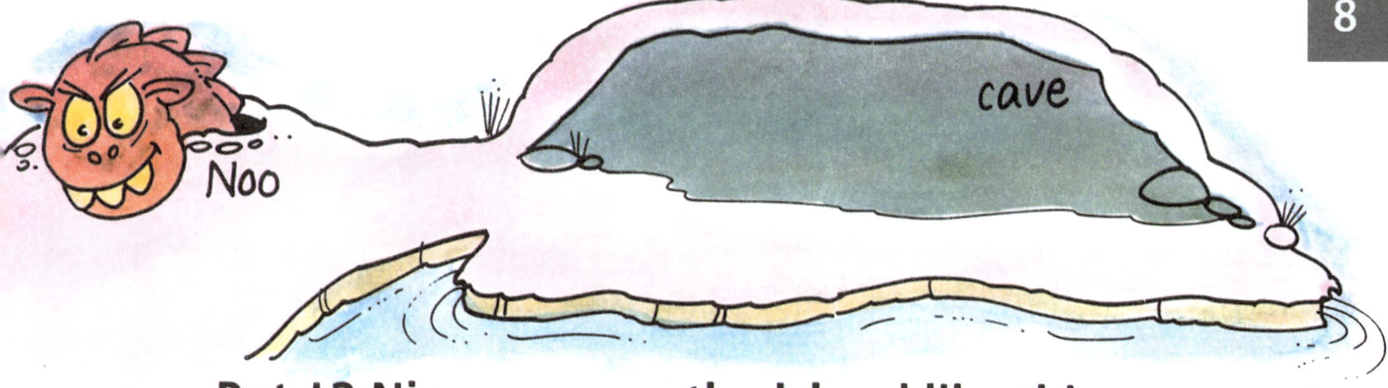

Put 12 Nim-nams on the island like this.

$$5 + 4 + 3 = 12$$

Find other ways.

$$\square + \square + \square = 12$$

$$\square + \square + \square = 12$$

$$\square + \square + \square = 12$$

Put 12 Nim-nams on the island.

If Noo eats 5, how many are left?

$$12 - 5 = \square$$

$$12 - 9 = \square \qquad 12 - 4 = \square \qquad 12 - 10 = \square$$

$$12 - 7 = \square \qquad 12 - 6 = \square \qquad 12 - 3 = \square$$

R22

Nim-nams

$7 + 5 =$

$5 + 7 =$

$12 - 5 =$

$12 - 7 =$

$9 + 3 =$

$3 + 9 =$

$12 - 3 =$

$12 - 9 =$

$8 + 4 =$

$4 + 8 =$

$12 - 4 =$

$12 - 8 =$

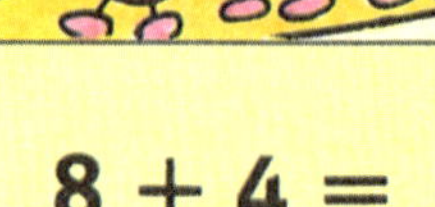

$6 + 6 =$

$12 - 6 =$

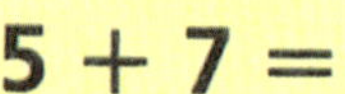

Nim-nam house

Find the answers.   Colour them.

red $7 + 3$ $12 - 10$ $12 - 7$

blue $12 - 4$ $8 + 3$ $6 + 6$

green $6 + 3$ $12 - 9$ $12 - 8$

How many altogether?

$$5 + 6$$

$$8 + 4$$

$$7 + 5$$

$$3 + 9$$

$$5 + 7$$

$$6 + 6$$

$$3 + 4 + 5$$

$$6 + 4 + 2$$

$$4 + 4 + 3$$

11

Bear Island

In each cave,
colour **three** bears that add to make 12.

The school cave has

an even answer greater than 10.

Write **School** above the school cave.

Use these numbers to make the sums.

9 8 4 3

Fun Island

Use 13 counters.

$$6 + 7$$

$$+$$

Find other stories for 13.

$+$	$+$	$+$	$+$	$+$	$+$
13	13	13	13	13	13

$$2 + 3 + 8 = 13$$

Find more stories like this for 13.

$6 + 7 = 13$

$7 + 6 =$

$13 - 6 =$

$13 - 7 =$

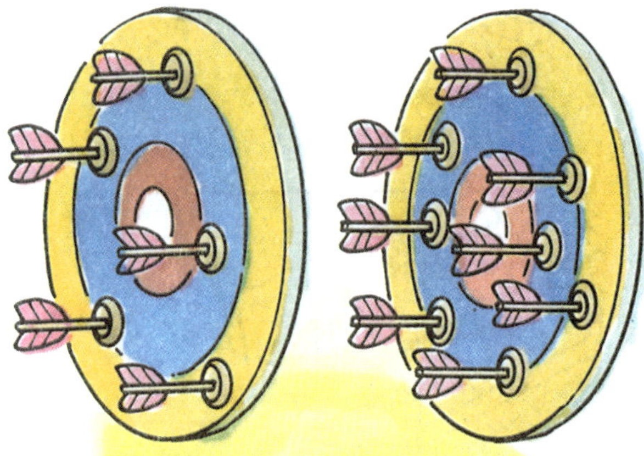

$5 + 8 =$

$8 + 5 =$

$13 - 5 =$

$13 - 8 =$

$9 + 4 =$

$4 + 9 =$

$13 - 9 =$

$13 - 4 =$

$10 + 3 =$

$3 + 10 =$

$13 - 10 =$

$13 - 3 =$

R 24

Train ride

Colour a carriage to match each answer.

R 25

Spooky Castle

Write the missing number.

7   9   11

This key opens the door.

13 children go in.
8 come out.

How many
are still in? ___

Add to find the one that is different.

6   6   8
5   7   5

**The trapdoor
key is in it.**

Escape

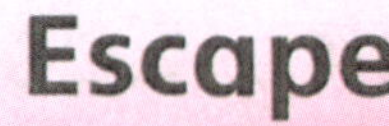

Write the answers.

$7 + 6 =$

$4 + 8 =$

$12 - 3 =$

$13 - 4 =$

$11 - 9 =$

$7 + 4 =$

$11 - 4 =$

$12 - 6 =$

$13 - 6 =$

Colour the boxes

blue   if the answer is odd,

red   if the answer is even.

Which door has an even answer? Colour it red.

Amy had 13p.
She lost 7p in the sea.

How much is left? ___ p

**Colour the monster that has two more
black spots than green spots.**

**Find chests with the same answer.
Colour them to match.**

**The treasure is in
the white chest.
Mark it ✗ .**

R 26

Find the cost of a fox and a bear . ___

Find the cost of a fox, a tiger and a dog . ___

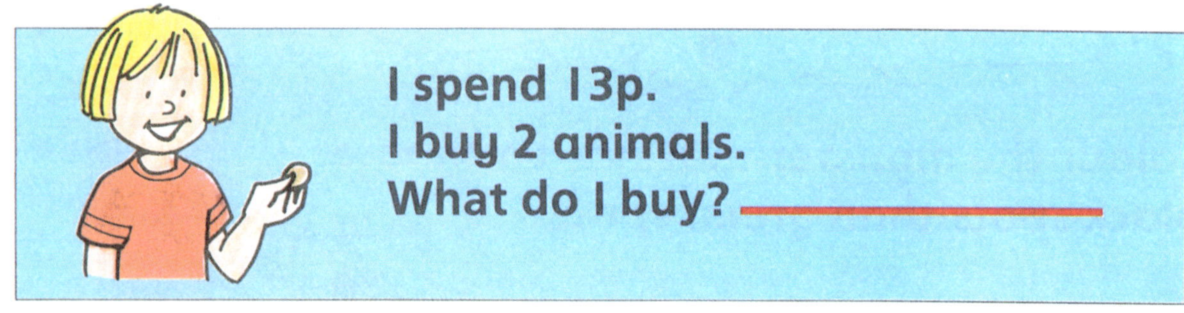

R 27

Prizes

8. + 7 =

15. − 6 =

 **Now do these.**

7 + 9 = ☐   6 + 8 = ☐   10 + 9 = ☐

16 − 7 = ☐   14 − 8 = ☐   17 − 9 = ☐

Who wins a prize? (✓)

Halves

Colour one half of each shape.

Tick the shapes that show halves.

Making halves

Cut out the four-strip. 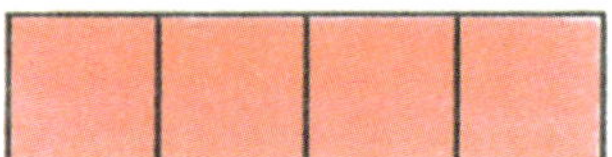

Fold it in half. 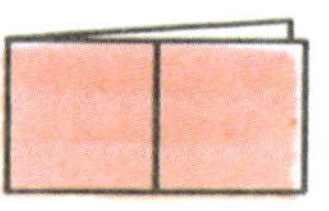

One half of 4 is ____ .

Cut out the six-strip. 

Fold it in half.

One half of 6 is ____ .

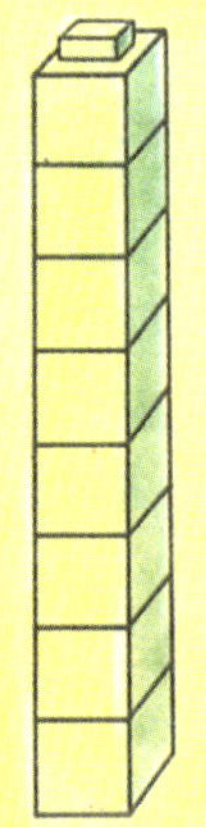

Make a tower with 8 cubes.

Halve it like this ⟶ 

One half of 8 is ____ .

Use 10 cubes.

One half of 10 is ____ .

Use cubes.　One half of 12 is ____ .

One half of 16 is ____ .

One half of 20 is ____ .

Quarters

You need

Fold each in quarters.

Colour one quarter of each shape.

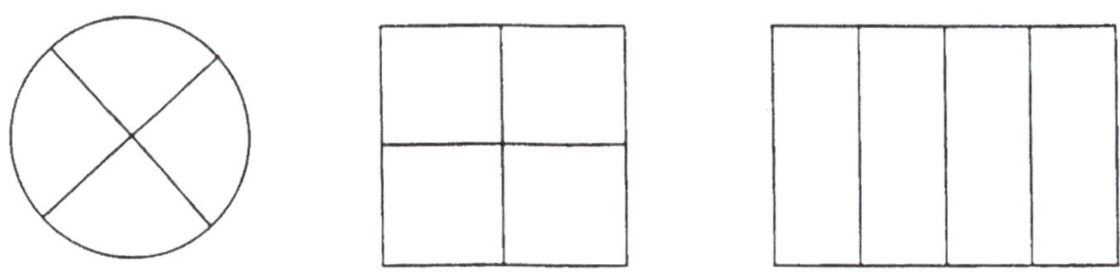

Tick the shapes that show quarters.

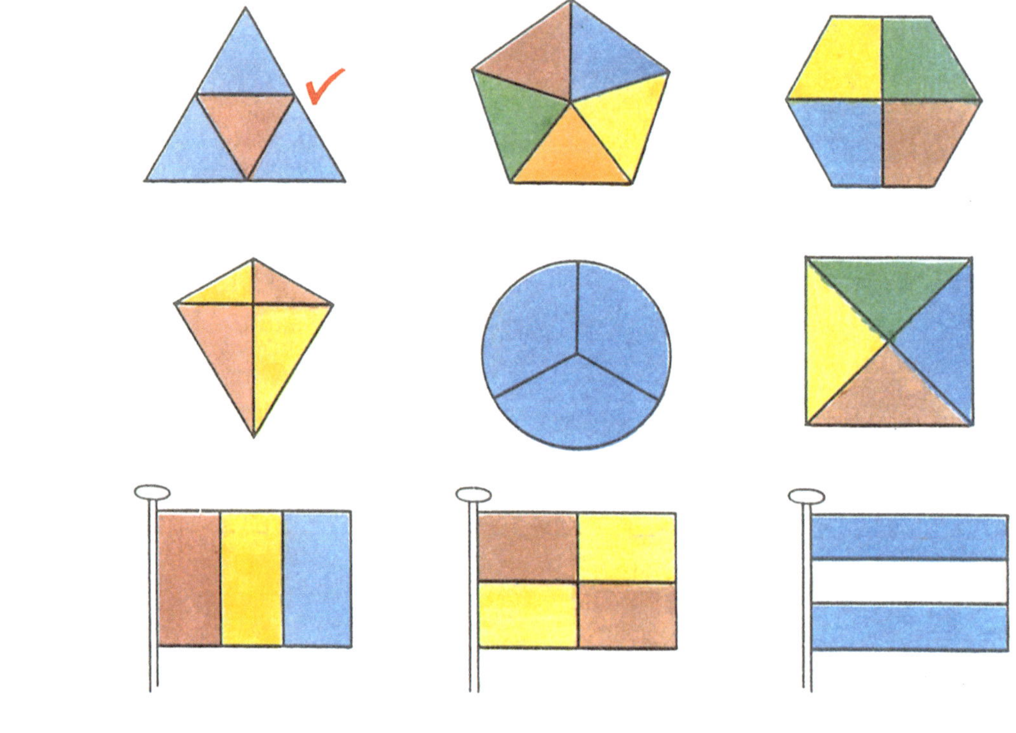

1	2	3	4	5	6	7	8	9	10	11	12	13	14	15	16	17	18	19	20	21	22	23

Heinemann is an imprint of Pearson Education Limited, a company incorporated in England and Wales, having its registered office at Edinburgh Gate, Harlow, Essex, CM20 2JE. Registered company number: 872828
ISBN 978 0 435 03094 0 © Scottish Primary Mathematics Group 1981.
First published 1991. Revised edition 1995.   25   32
Typeset and Illustrated by Oxprint Design. Printed in Great Britain by Bell & Bain Ltd, Glasgow

ISBN 978-0-435030-94-0
9 780435 030940